Apostolic Reinforcement to Strengthen the Church

SIMEON J. FRAZIER, SR.

(Apostolic Reinforcement to Strengthen the Church)
Copyright © 2016 by (Simeon J. Frazier, Sr.)

Unless otherwise indicated, all scriptural quotations are from the New King James Version of the Bible copyright 1982 by Thomas Nelson, Inc.

ISBN 13: 978-1532910999

Table of Contents

Dedication

This book is dedicated to my mother, the late Priscilla Mae Frazier, through her prayers, her love for God, people, and her support and faith in me as her son and a man of God. This book is dedicated in her memory, because she encouraged me daily in the things of God. Mom, I know the Lord is letting you see what I am doing to expand His kingdom on Earth.

Acknowledgement

To Bishop Randy Spencer, thank you for demonstrating the love of God during my valley times.

To Priscilla Potts, thank you for lifting my spirit with your words of wisdom. It has challenged me to after my vision no matter what I face.

To Deacon Reggie Landrum, thank you for being a spiritual son for REAL.

To Prophetess Jamila N. Marshall, founder of Dan~Zing 4 Him Outreach Ministries, Inc., thank you for your constant encouragement, inspiration, and motivation. May our Heavenly Father continue to increase your ministry and vision worldwide.

Introduction

The Restoration of an Apostolic Ministry brings a great manifestation of the spirit of God on the Earth. The church needs help to be what God is calling it to be in these last days. This is why there is Apostolic Reinforcement.

The word "reinforce" in the Webster's dictionary is defined as: to strengthen or increase by fresh additions. The church needs strengthen and fresh revelations to increase in this season of the spirit of God. I believe the Lord is raising up apostolic and prophetic ministries to bring the reinforcement. The church needs to move to ***new levels in God's Anointing***.

Chapter I
First Apostles

Now you are the body of Christ, and members individually. And God has appointed these in the church: first apostles, second prophets, third teachers, after that miracles, then gifts of healings, helps, administrations, varieties of tongues. ~
I Corinthians 12:27-28

Notice what verse 28 says, God has set in the church first apostles. It didn't say, man has set, it didn't say the people voted, it didn't say the Pastor's gift is first; the bible says first apostles!

The Greek word for the word "first", in this verse, is the word "proton". It means: first in time, first in place, first in order, before, beginning, foremost, and best. The Greek word for apostle is "apostolos", which means one who is sent, officially a commissioner of Christ.

For too long the church has been dependent on the gift of the Pastor and the gift of the Evangelist. These gifts are important, but, in these last days, God the father is honoring the office of the Apostle.

Apostles are here to give the church the reinforcement that we need to be a strong, Holy Spirit people full of the life and purpose of God; flowing out of our beings, glory to God!

God is a God of order. When the church violates the order of God, then the church is out of order. The bible says first apostles. Apostles must be at the beginning of any new thing that the Lord is doing on the Earth. Look at Acts 2:14-18 after the outpouring of the Holy Spirit. It reads:

14 But Peter, standing up with the eleven, raised his voice and said to them, "Men of Judea and all who dwell in Jerusalem, let this be known to you, and heed my words.

15 For these are not drunk, as you suppose, since it is only the third hour of the day.

16 But this is what was spoken by the prophet Joel:

17 And it shall come to pass in the last days, says God, That I will pour out of My Spirit on all flesh; Your sons and your daughters shall prophesy, Your young men shall see visions, Your old men shall dream dreams.

18 And on My menservants and on My maidservants I will pour out My Spirit in those days; And they shall prophesy.

Notice in verse 14 it says the Apostle Peter standing up with the other eleven apostles. And then Apostle Peter preached that nobody was drunk, because it was only the third hour of the day or nine o'clock in the morning. But this is the new thing that God is doing in the Earth. Be filled with the Holy Spirit!

The Greek word for standing is the word "**his temi**", it means to appoint, to covenant, establish, and continue.

If the church is going to be established in the new things of the Spirit of God, we need apostles.

If the church is going to experience all of the covenant blessings of the Gospel, we need apostles.

If the church is going to experience breakthroughs in our cities, we need apostles.

If the church want to see the gifts of the spirit flowing out of the lives of believers consistently, we need apostles.

The body of Christ must begin to embrace the ministry of the apostles, because of the reinforcement this anointing adds to the churches.

Let's look at some of the reinforcement the apostles bring to the church:

1. Impart spiritual gifts *(Romans 1:11)*.
2. Fullness of the blessing of the gospel of Christ *(Romans 15:29)*.
3. Impart the baptism of the Holy Spirit *(Acts 8:14-17)*.
4. Miracles *(Acts 19:11-12)*.
5. Apostles release an anointing through their preaching that helps the church breakthrough against demonic forces in cities, communities, and countries *(Acts 19:13-26)*.
6. Brings strength to the believers *(Acts 9:22)*. Apostles have compassion to see that believers are being strong in the Lord.

There are many other duties and functions of the apostles, but I wanted you to look at these six areas so that you can see for yourself that these things are lacking in the body of Christ. Thank God for the reinforcement of the ministry of the apostles being restored back in the church to add to and not take away from it.

Remember what they told Jesus in His days on Earth? The religious people of His day said, "You are not following the laws of Moses." Jesus said I came to fulfill the law; in other words, Jesus said I come to reinforce the law to **ADD TO**. That is what the apostle's ministry is to the church, not to destroy, but to **ADD TO** what the church is doing in the Earth, glory to God!

Notes

_____

_____

_____

_____

_____

_____

_____

_____

_____

_____

_____

Chapter Two
Signs of an Apostolic Church

One of the signs of an apostolic church is the manifestation of the five-fold ministry gifts. They are mentioned in Ephesians 4:11 it reads:

"And He Himself gave some to be apostles, some prophets, some evangelists, and some pastors and teachers, for the equipping of the saints for the work of ministry, for the edifying of the body of Christ."~ Ephesians 4:11-12

If the church is going to be perfected to do the work of the ministry, the needs to transition from the pastoral mindset, into an apostolic mindset. The word perfecting in verse 12 in the Greek is the word "**katartimos**", meaning "complete furnishing." When you buy a house, you buy the furniture to go in every room, even when you rent an apartment, you buy furniture to go in every room. What did you do? Every room was complete. Well guess what, if the church is not embracing all five gifts that are mentioned in verse 11, then the church is not complete. Thank God for the restoration of the five-fold ministry gifts being accepted and perfected in the body of Christ.

The only gifts that the church has been trained to accept is the pastor, evangelist, and teacher. We need all five gifts if we are to be a complete people. Pastors, if God is not calling you to the office of an apostle, you need to invite an apostle into your church at least on a quarterly basis. This will release an apostolic anointing into your church. Pastors, you need to put yourself into an apostolic network. This will release an apostolic dimension in your life and in the life of the people you are leading. Apostles will help pastors release and activate prophets and prophetess in the local church. Pastors, you need prophets in your church. Their gifts are important, just like your teachers and evangelists. Apostolic reinforcement will help churches manifest five-fold gifting in local churches in these last days, like no other time in church history. I will talk about how to release the five-fold in your church more in Chapter Five on the Apostolic and Prophetic Conferences.

Other signs of an apostolic church:
1. Reformation preaching and teaching (*Hebrews 9:10*). The Greek word for reformation is "diorthosis," meaning straighten thoroughly, rectification. Apostolic reinforcement preaching and teaching helps straighten out things in the church that are out of order.

2. Strong anointing of activating the gifts of the Holy Spirit (*2 Timothy 1:6*).

3. Resistance from demons, religious, and traditional systems *(Ephesians 6:10-12)*.

4. Angelic assistance *(Acts 5:17-20, 12:5-11)*.

5. Walk in the fear of the Lord *(Acts 9:31)*.

6. Prophets and Prophetess will be known and released to prophesy in the local church *(Acts 11:27-30, 13:1, 15:27-33, 21:8-12)*.

7. Signs, wonders, and miracles will occur (Mark 16:15-18).

Notes

Chapter Three
Apostolic Foundation

"Now, therefore, you are no longer strangers and foreigners, but fellow citizens with the saints and members of the household of God, [20] having been built on the foundation of the apostles and prophets, Jesus Christ Himself being the chief cornerstone." ~ Ephesians 2:19-20

The word foundation in the Greek is the word **"themelios,"** meaning a substructure of a building. Substructure of a building is the underlying or supporting part of a structure. In other words, NO foundation, NO building. The foundation is the underlying base or support. Buildings are built on the foundation. Schools are built on foundation. The foundation is the FIRST THING that goes into the ground.

The church was built upon the foundation of the apostles and prophets. Jesus Christ being the chief cornerstone. In other words, Jesus started the building (the church). In addition, he gave the apostles and prophets the ability to lay down the structure (building of the church).

Most of the foundation that the apostles imparted to the church are being neglected by religion and tradition. BUT, thank God for the restoration of true Apostolic

Doctrine being brought back to the church. We need the preaching and teaching of apostolic current truth.

Most preaching we hear on the radio and television is to get the believer to shout and dance. Ninety percent of the time, the messages seem to say:

"Hold On. Hold Fast. God is bringing you through! He won't forget you, be still, and praise him! He's your doctor! He's your lawyer! He's your keeper!"

If believers keep on hearing messages like that, the church will not be empowered to get the power of the Holy Spirit to do great exploits for God.

The church must began to build upon the foundation of the apostles and prophets that the Lord is raising up in these last days. If the church is going to be a glorious church without spot or wrinkle, then the church needs reinforcement of apostolic foundation. This will keep the church vibrant, excited, loving, and anointed. Apostolic foundation will release ministry gifts in a local church. Also, apostolic foundation will release ministry gifts to nations.

Remember, foundation is the beginning structure of apostolic and prophetic foundation and can foresee the needs of the church. Let's look at Acts 2: 41-43:

41Then those who gladly received his word were baptized; and that day about three thousand souls were added to them. 42 And they continued steadfastly in the apostles' doctrine and fellowship, in the breaking of bread, and in prayers. 43 Then fear came upon every soul, and many wonders and signs were done through the apostles.

The early church received the word from Apostle Peter. They continued in the word of the apostles, because they kept the foundation of the apostles' teachings. The apostles were released to work signs, wonders, and miracles. You see, the foundation was laid. It was easy for the apostles to flow in signs and wonders, because the people believed in their teachings. If the church wants to move to the next level of signs and wonders, I believe, the church must begin to embrace true apostles in which the Lord is raising up in this hour.

Apostolic foundational reinforcement to the church will help the church:

1. Be strong in the Lord (Ephesians 6:10).

2. Revelations and mysteries of the word to open up to the church (Ephesians 3:3-5).

3. Current truth (Ephesians 4:11-14).

4. Ordain the right people and set them in their right office of ministry (I Timothy 3:1-14).

5. Plant churches in tough areas (Ephesians 2:20).

Notes

_____

_____

_____

_____

_____

_____

_____

_____

_____

_____

_____

Chapter Four
Apostolic Anointing

"Then Jesus returned in the power of the Spirit to Galilee, and news of Him went out through all the surrounding region" ~ *Luke 4:14*

"The Spirit of the Lord is upon Me, because He has anointed Me to preach the gospel to the poor; He has sent Me to heal the brokenhearted, to proclaim liberty to the captives and recovery of sight to the blind, to set at liberty those who are oppressed." ~ *Luke 4:18*

Jesus walked in the power of the spirit of God or the anointing of the Spirit of God. Jesus released or imparted the same apostolic anointing to His apostles when he sent them out to do ministry. Look at *Luke 9:1-2*:

"Then He called His twelve disciples together and gave them power and authority over all demons, and to cure diseases. He sent them to preach the kingdom of God and to heal the sick."

Apostles have received an anointing from Jesus to manifest Jesus on Earth. This same anointing is released to the believers through apostles so that believers will operate in a strong apostolic spirit. The apostolic anointing flows from Jesus through the apostles to the believers.

When apostles come to your city, preach at your church, or if apostles pastor churches, they come with the fullness of the anointing. Look at *Romans 15:29*, listen to the words of the Apostle Paul:

"But I know that when I come to you, I shall come in the fullness of the blessing of the gospel of Christ."

In route to Rome from Corinth, the Apostle Paul wrote the believers saying, "When I get there to your city, I will bring in the fullness of the blessings of the gospel." Glory to God! In other words, Paul said, I am coming with the fullness of the anointed one and His anointing.

Paul was a representative of Christ, saying whatever is in the **Christ**, the anointed one, I am anointed to impart into you, GLORY! Thank God for the apostles God is raising up in this last day to release an apostolic anointing upon the church.

Here are a list of five things you will see happening in the church when there is an apostolic anointing present:

1. Praise and Worship will move to a greater degree of deliverance and the songs will tear down demonic strongholds. See *Acts 16:25-31*

2. The Church will become more apostolic in the preaching. Most messages being

preached on Sundays are encouraging believers to "hold on", "hold fast", and "Jesus will make a way." The apostolic anointing will push you to do ministry in spite of opposition. See *Acts 8:1-4* (The apostolic anointing encourages sending not holding.)

3. Prophetic Utterances and personal prophecy will become frequent. See *I Thessalonians 5:19-20*

4. The church will have a team approach to ministry instead of the one man approach. Apostles and the apostolic anointing releases believers into their assigned place in the church See *I Timothy 4:14*

5. The gifts of the Holy Spirit will be manifested through the believers not just the pastor or the church leaders. See *I Corinthians 12:1-13*

Apostles carry the grace to release the apostolic anointing into the body of Christ. The church needs the reinforcement of the apostolic anointing, if it is going to experience end-times victories over Satan.

Notes

Chapter Five
Apostolic and Prophetic Conferences

"Now in the church that was at Antioch there were certain prophets and teachers: Barnabas, Simeon who was called Niger, Lucius of Cyrene, Manaen who had been brought up with Herod the tetrarch, and Saul. As they ministered to the Lord and fasted, the Holy Spirit said, "Now separate to Me Barnabas and Saul for the work to which I have called them." ~Acts 13:1-2

Most conferences the church has been used to for years is to have popular speakers, singers, and choirs. This will draw in the people and the money. Believers leave the conference excited for a moment, but there is something missing. I know what is missing! There was not an apostolic anointing present. The apostolic anointing release signs, wonders, and exploits for the glory of God! In Acts the 13th chapter, the apostolic leaders came together- apostles, prophets, and teachers- to minister to the Lord at this gathering. The apostolic anointing was released upon the leaders to send two of them **Out!**

Apostolic conferences will release believers into their destiny. At apostolic conferences, believers will be ministered to by teams of prophets and apostles. It's not like your traditional conferences where one man speaks and **THAT'S IT- GO HOME, NO!** Apostolic conferences will give the church impartation and activation of the gifts of the spirit in the lives of the believers.

Apostolic conferences will take the time to minister prophetically. Apostolic and Prophetic conferences will help churches establish five-fold ministry gifts in the local church by the personal prophetic ministry, corporate prophetic ministry, and by having apostolic and prophetic teams established at the conference.

The workshops at apostolic conferences will help bring fresh additions to the church. Remember one of the definitions for "reinforcement" is to add fresh additions.

Here is a list of some of the workshops you will get the opportunity to attend that is offered through Apostolic Training Academy:

- Pastoral to the Apostolic
- Spiritual Sons & Daughters Flowing in the Apostolic Anointing
- First Apostles, Second Prophets
- Apostolic Warfare
- Prophetic Ministry
- The Tabernacle of David
- How to set up Apostolic and Prophetic Teams
- Reformation, the Key to Transitioning Out of Tradition

These are just some of the workshops that you will have the opportunity to attend at the apostolic conference. There are much, much more topics to discuss.

Remember the apostolic move of God, in these last days, is not to take away from the church, but to add to the church. Some will try to fight the change, but man cannot fight what God has ordained for this hour in the church. Apostolic reinforcement is here until Jesus comes.

For Speaking Engagements:

If you would like Simeon J. Frazier, Sr. to speak at one of your events, you can email the administration office at atmosphershift1278@gmail.com. Leave a detailed message of your event, date, time, and city and state and our Administration Staff will contact you soon.

Made in the USA
Columbia, SC
29 August 2017